SAFARI

Kangaroos

by Kari Schuetz

BLASTOFF! READERS

BELLWETHER MEDIA • MINNEAPOLIS, MN

Note to Librarians, Teachers, and Parents:

Blastoff! Readers are carefully developed by literacy experts and combine standards-based content with developmentally appropriate text.

Level 1 provides the most support through repetition of high-frequency words, light text, predictable sentence patterns, and strong visual support.

Level 2 offers early readers a bit more challenge through varied simple sentences, increased text load, and less repetition of high-frequency words.

Level 3 advances early-fluent readers toward fluency through increased text and concept load, less reliance on visuals, longer sentences, and more literary language.

Level 4 builds reading stamina by providing more text per page, increased use of punctuation, greater variation in sentence patterns, and increasingly challenging vocabulary.

Level 5 encourages children to move from "learning to read" to "reading to learn" by providing even more text, varied writing styles, and less familiar topics.

Whichever book is right for your reader, Blastoff! Readers are the perfect books to build confidence and encourage a love of reading that will last a lifetime!

This edition first published in 2013 by Bellwether Media, Inc.

No part of this publication may be reproduced in whole or in part without written permission of the publisher. For information regarding permission, write to Bellwether Media, Inc., Attention: Permissions Department, 5357 Penn Avenue South, Minneapolis, MN 55419.

Library of Congress Cataloging-in-Publication Data
Schuetz, Kari.
Kangaroos / by Kari Schuetz.
  p. cm. – (Blastoff! readers: animal safari)
Audience: 4-8.
Audience: K to grade 3.
Summary: "Developed by literacy experts for students in kindergarten through grade three, this book introduces kangaroos to young readers through leveled text and related photos"– Provided by publisher.
Includes bibliographical references and index.
ISBN 978-1-60014-864-4 (hardcover : alk. paper)
1. Kangaroos–Juvenile literature. I. Title.
QL737.M35S38 2013
599.2'22–dc23   2012031229

Printed in the United States of America, North Mankato, MN.

Contents

What Are Kangaroos?

Kangaroos are large **marsupials** with big feet.

They hop to move.
Their powerful legs
can carry them
30 feet (9 meters)
in one leap!

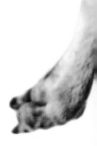

Their strong tails help them **balance** and turn.

Mobs in the Outback

Kangaroos live in the **outback**. They **graze** on grasslands.

They travel in **mobs** of 50 or more. Males lead the mobs.

Males **box** with one another. They fight for females.

Females care for **joeys**. They keep joeys safe inside their belly **pouches**.

pouch

Staying Safe

Kangaroos warn one another of danger. They thump the ground with their feet if they spot **predators**.

They kick dingoes
that come too
close. Hiya!

Glossary

balance—to stay steady and not fall

box—to fight with the fists

graze—to feed on grasses and other plants

joeys—baby kangaroos

marsupials—animals that carry their young inside belly pouches

mobs—groups of kangaroos that live and travel together

outback—the wild countryside of Australia

pouches—pockets on the bellies of female marsupials; joeys stay inside these pouches.

predators—animals that hunt other animals for food

To Learn More

AT THE LIBRARY

Bredeson, Carmen. *Kangaroos Up Close.* Berkeley Heights, N.J.: Enslow Elementary, 2009.

Costain, Meredith. *My Life in the Wild: Kangaroo.* New York, N.Y.: Kingfisher, 2012.

Lunis, Natalie. *Red Kangaroo: The World's Largest Marsupial.* New York, N.Y.: Bearport, 2010.

ON THE WEB
Learning more about kangaroos is as easy as 1, 2, 3.

1. Go to www.factsurfer.com.

2. Enter "kangaroos" into the search box.

3. Click the "Surf" button and you will see a list of related Web sites.

With factsurfer.com, finding more information is just a click away.

Index

The images in this book are reproduced through the courtesy of: imagebroker.net/SuperStock, front cover; Carolina Garcia Aranda, p. 5; Martin Zwick/Age Fotostock, p. 7; J & C Sohns/Age Fotostock, p. 9; Martin Harvey/KimballStock, p. 11; NHPA/SuperStock, p. 13; Steve Bloom Images/SuperStock, p. 15; M Willemeit/Age Fotostock, p. 17; Ted Mead/Getty Images, p. 19; Gerry Pearce/Alamy, p. 21 (left); Mitsuaki Iwago/Minden Pictures, p. 21 (right).